FRUITFLY
GEOGRAPHIC

STEPHEN BROCKWELL

E C W
MISFIT
PRESS

Published by ECW PRESS
2120 Queen Street East, Suite 200, Toronto, Ontario, Canada M4E 1E2

NATIONAL LIBRARY OF CANADA CATALOGUING IN PUBLICATION

Brockwell, Stephen
Fruitfly geographic / Stephen Brockwell.

Poems.
ISBN 1-55022-647-9

I. Title.

PS8553.R6135F78 2004   C811'.54   C2003-907292-4
A misFit book

Editor: Michael Holmes / a misFit book
Cover and Text Design: Darren Holmes
Cover photo: rob mclennan
Production and Typesetting: Mary Bowness
Printing: Gauvin Press

This book is set in Goudy.

The publication of *Fruitfly Geographic* has been generously supported by the Canada Council, the Ontario Arts Council, the Ontario Media Development Corporation, and the Government of Canada through the Book Publishing Industry Development Program. **Canadä**

DISTRIBUTION
CANADA: Jaguar Book Group, 100 Armstrong Avenue, Georgetown, ON, L7G 5S4

PRINTED AND BOUND IN CANADA

ECW PRESS
ecwpress.com

FRUITFLY
GEOGRAPHIC

"... electronic man is no less a nomad
than his Palaeolithic ancestors."
—Marshall McLuhan

CONTENTS

Evolutions

Fruitfly Geographic

DART

I've spent half my life
　　　　learning to play darts
in the dark. To find
　　　　the sharp point without
bleeding was the first
　　　　lesson. To measure
distances by the dart's
　　　　thud in the wood
paneling downstairs
　　　　or by the skitter
of feathers on the
　　　　linoleum floor
was the second.
　　　　If I could see the target
I'd toss three triple
　　　　twenties with such ease
the tournaments of England
　　　　would invite me.
But I confess—and this
　　　　darkness has been
a long forestalling
　　　　of confession—
there never was a target
　　　　I could see
but a tree of targets
　　　　for a single dart.
Or was the target a
　　　　Baffin Island hut
abandoned, say,
　　　　a hundred years ago?

TRIP REPORTS

Montreal

The taxi driver
smokes. Minus 30. His bare
hand carries my bags.

Hands of the Father

One hundred thousand hours of paper,
printer's ink and penciled estimates
have shaped his hands,
fingers sturdy as walking sticks.
On weekends they became instruments
for tying knots he could not name:
a clove-hitch supported the fences
when pasture thinned and cattle
stretched the page wire; a bowline
steadied the TV antenna in gusts
that crossed the field; twin cat's paws
pulled his car doors together.

Their ancestry lies
in the hands of his father,
a merchant seaman who lies
in Bermuda, the charitable dairyman
of the great depression,
a bankrupt who left for sea
when his son was eight years old, whose hands
are a memory from a photograph.

To secure a calf for branding,
my father tied a random knot
of endless loops and bends,
a mystery neither sailor
nor mathematician could unravel.
This was his knot of knots:
a victory for the hands of the father

who holds his shining
radiated head, right hand
stroking his scalp for warmth, left hand

releasing comforting drops
until he says he has to go.

Sixty-four years of heat
dissipate through his hands.
They are laid to rest in his lap.

PENANG

Bird song, cinnamon, fatigue, the flight
memorable for its lack of sleep.
Daiquiris in the Honolulu lounge
in transit, biting stalks
of celery. Breakfast
at the hotel—a feast of peppers,
turmeric and chicken.
Start the day with a tongue of fire,
a final presentation to deaf
but fluent-in-English ears.
Decline an invitation to a Kuala Lumpur
dance hall; take, full of sleep, the short
flight to Penang.
Three nights of night markets:
masks, batik shirts, gamelan,
open fires, German and English
tourists, a red and yellow sarong
brought home in the hope
that my wife will wear it. The last day:
a walk in Georgetown where a rickshaw
driver sits with the back of his head
in the clasped palms of his hands,
wearing a pair of shorts, smiling
in front of his shack where the chickens
surround him, well fed from the open
sewers. A clay pot of squid, star
anise and long beans. A torrent of rain
the chef washes her hands in.

Blue Bonnets

Does a mare
pummel the turf
with her hooves
or is her gait—
the counter-weight
canter of the sulky
the full-throttle
gallop of the flailed
furlong—a strategy?

Go from
gate to ribbon;
limit the whip.

My grandfather's moist hand
vacillates.
Where to place his last $2 bill—
on Bohemian Sapphire
in the 10th,
or Bombay Sapphire
in the Schweppes?

Meditation on the Cold from the Home Office

To survive the Canadian winter
you must remember the black flies of spring.
Walking home over a bridge at evening,
the wind slaps your face numb like a drunken
father; your breath freezes on your eyelashes.
Naked under wool overcoat and trousers,
looking down at the snow on the railway,
you wonder how it would be to walk there
in a T-shirt, unaware of your breathing,
the green hair of the earth beside the tracks.
You almost forget there would be a gravel
railway bed. You say "gravel," you say "grass."
Before late January, your friends fled
to Belize to wash their feet in sea foam
along that stretch of shell and coral snow,
preferring not to remember. You walk
on stale green. In shirtsleeves, a bus driver
kneels beside a shivering woman who
lies on the ice, half-covered by his coat,
collapsed outside the Curry Corner Tavern.
Hazard lights flash on her tongue; tail pipe fumes
gather, greet her like a returning guest.

ABANDONED PUMP HOUSE CLEANING

The nostrils girded for the shock
of mildew, turds, and cat piss
under the fibreglass insulation
(as, at the Highland Games, I grappled

with my father in a tug-of-war,
stiffening my body until the rope stiffened,
and he let go, hurtling me into the grass).
Instead, the eyes witnessed the patina

of years of bronze urine, clusters
of obsidian feces, the mummified body
of a field mouse that survived
winter's sub-zero and the barn's starving cats.

AUKLAND

Fist-sized mussels, wine to make them
blush in New South Wales,
lamb that must have been butchered
yesterday, a client
free from preconceptions
and budget approval. Having won
in principle, endure the perfect
weather and from the bar see their neon
corporate logo illuminate the city
like a broken promise. Who will explain
the photographs of our dancing?
Convinced by dusk
we will drink with the Maori
rugby players until dawn,
ask the band to play less
American blues. By midnight we have
each learned a new and different language.
Forgetting our tongues in our glasses,
we utter names and leave
subtle communication
to grimaces and uncomfortable
gestures of the hand.
Only the loudspeakers,
cracking John Lee Hooker,
require no translation,
as close as we will come
to the Queen's English.

FIELD CHURNING

The irony of colour
expressed an accidental butter:
running over the fields,
I churned a jar of fresh cream;
the sun aligned the fat and ripened it.
Not even the chilled copper kettle
could cool it white; the eggbeaters
clotted with its summer.
My father said, "If it's not sweet enough
for pie, salt it for the corn,"
skim milk and butter dripping from his chin.

Head Office Update: Shortcut

No shortcut in Marin county.
This path leads to
abandoned tracks,
gullies,
a white great blue heron,
vultures over a hare,
a walk back
$^1/_4$ mile to the freeway exit.
Put no faith in flowers and reeds—they are no sign of passage.
Where the vultures thought and dined
only a blotch of blood remains—
a spilled Sonoma syrah.
A 68-year-old woman drives by in a '72 Beetle
the hair on the back of my neck
standing.

Swarming

At least a thousand wings—
each lighter and thinner than the callus shavings
we curled with a razor from our twine-hardened
fingers—hummed like a James Bay transmission line,

stopped our crew from hauling in the hay,
silenced five sun- and sweat-anointed boys.
A bronze golem, the hive strode over the wagon
and the barn roof from an origin

we looked for (and thought we'd found, later,
in the hollow trunk of a lightning-cracked maple)
to a destination we never dreamed of looking for.

Accepting the wineskin filled with Coke and Alcool,
I kept to myself that two bees had lit on my arm
but that I hadn't dared move or scream.

NAGOYA

Sleep in the small, hard
beds with 300 thread-per-inch sheets.
Buy heated, canned
espresso from a vending machine
on the street. Bless the interpreter:
so many streets; no
sign recognizable
without instruction. Sip
while the client confers
in the smoke-filled boardroom.
Pre-fabricated sushi for lunch
found in a mall that floods our ears
with American Christmas classics.
At 6:00 p.m. team-build
at a private pub—
Asahi flows, but in what pub
is there a pizza of shredded dried
shark? Duck under the door of a fish
grill house where the sake
overflows the cup into a tray. Drink
from both. Point, "That one!"
They love to laugh at us and we
are happy they are laughing.
Only when Craig, having
eaten the barely cooked
liver of the mackerel, falls
from his chair, eyes
streaming, full of stars, do we
wish that one of us speaks Japanese, or that,
by god, the cook perhaps speaks
French.

EST

My father will never taste the finest wine;
grown in an abandoned Tuscan vineyard,
it matured in clay before the birth of Christ.
He will never caress the softest skin;
it belonged to a nun who would never
reconcile her virtue with her beauty.
He will never be moved
by the most beautiful song; it was sung
to put a wakeful child to sleep, the mother
never wrote it down. His eyes will never
fall on the most symmetrical rose;
it has yet to be planted. Somewhere
new genes for it are being conceived.
I will never read the perfect poem; it was
written by a poet who discovered
her tongue before her tongue discovered her.
It burned on a pyre of books in Berlin.
Words, exhausted from too much talk, retire
from perfection. We will sleep perfectly.

Meditation on the Spheres
from the Home Office

Before we covered this sphere with countless
clamouring bodies, with steel and concrete
containers connected by ribbons
of bitumen and crushed gravel, how far
would a voice travel? Across what distance
could I address you clearly above the din
of traffic bringing mothers home from work,
of clinking wine glasses and arguments.
Let me try. Stand this book on your bed,
the poem vertical, the spine supporting
securely this page. From the corner of the room,
read these words aloud, child and dog asleep,
alarm clock muffled under the pillow.
There will be a moment when a car does not pass,
when a passenger jet does not fly.
The breeze brushes the spruce. You can almost
hear the collisions of clouds as quiet
in their path across the Earth as the planets
in their orbits. Proving the greatest gifts
are silently given, you hear your breath.

HEAD OFFICE UPDATE: GECKO, FLOWERS

What's the gecko doing
near the rock? Dressed
in simple skin, colour-matched with dust,
anonymity is its end but hawks
see it. Colourless
it moves and movement too
catches the eye
much as the minute yellow
blossoms of these weeds
cracking the sidewalk
cry like babies,
"O visit me, bees!"

TORONTO

An unmarried man
would write other lines; he would
have less time for notes.

Step Dance

I stepped up on a stair
at the back of our house;
the stair countered my weight
with the resistance
of concrete and wood.

I stepped on a rock
in a dry riverbed;
the rock turned under my ankle
as a shovel
turns to spill sand.

I stepped onto a train
for Montreal
and walked up the aisle; the train
pushed me to my meeting
ahead of schedule.

I stepped on a root
of an ash in bloom
and felt the root anchored in earth,
limb of a tree the wind
could not move easily.

I danced on my father's ashes.

VISITS TO
MUSEUMS

Three Deaths of Hippasus of Metapontum

Vertex, Leaving

To think it was one thing,
to say it, another; you could have breathed
for years
thinking it.

Edge

Hippasus, soaked by secrets,
legend has it
you drowned in a fisherman's dream of the sea.
A leak in the boat
had a hand in your death.
The hands raised the boat
by the ballast of your body.
Pythagoras downcast
wept at the necessary end
by sufficient means,
flayed, until blood stained the sand,
his back, kneaded his face with salt.
The truth is no ratio of the squares
of two natural numbers equals two.
How did the thought root in your mind?
Say a couple in the cove surf
double joy
for square miles of sea. No fish perceive
their ecstasy; swimming
among seaweed near the reef,
the school sees the nameless
colours of the coral.
Accept the fact of this
and even the cove
teems with odd eels.

Vertex, Entering

Not to know it in the scrawl of a pencil
but to taste its truth on the original tongue
align the pebbles in the dust,
reckon the shapes, kneeling.

Vertex, Leaving

Not to think it in the familiar notation
but to think of it
swallow the language of the dead,
spit out the mother tongue.

Edge

Hippasus, seared by secrets,
legend has it
you choked on a poisoned pit in the heat of eating.
Space in the courtyard
had been made for your grave.
The school had a hand
digging it from the hard earth of Croton.
Pythagoras crestfallen
wept at the sufficient means
for the necessary end,
tore the white remains of his hair,
polished his scalp with dust.
The truth is the square of no ratio
of two natural numbers equals two.
How did the belief grow in your mind?
Say the sun simmers an olive grove
for hectares. Harvesters
loosen the fruit from the stems
with sticks. Fled from the grove,

olive warblers, shy birds, never see
the overflowing baskets, speckling
the grove with green.
Believe this
and even the grove
fills with odd crows.

VERTEX, ENTERING

You measured three squares
of a triangle
from pebbles in the sand
aligned to a carpenter's rule.

VERTEX, LEAVING

You transcribed the script
of a new language
from the palimpsest
of pebbles in the sand.

EDGE

Hippasus, cooled by secrets,
legend has it
you expired in your bed with a summer breeze.
Your daughter's hands
closed your eyes, full of sight.
The hair on your hands
grew, long after your burial.
Pythagoras deceased may have
wept at his insufficient means
for the necessary end, may have
cursed the path you wandered out on.
The truth is no natural number squared equals
twice another natural number squared.

How did the proof bloom in your mind?
Say a heavy metal, cradled
in a magnetic field, waits
for the neutron to drop.
White coats with instruments
measure the imaginary aspect
of one or the other measurement
no transcendental number quantifies.
The first use of this dream
makes air from flesh with fire.
The second use of this dream
makes fire from earth with water
to illuminate Manhattan
where the distance between
Liberty and Church and
Vesey and West Side Highway
is exactly two blocks.
The truth of an utterance is proved
by the untimely death of its first speaker.
Pythagoras never spoke it.
Even the odd temple fills.

Vertex, Entering

To prove it was one thing,
to speak it, another; did you wander
for years
reproving it?

PARTHENON STALLION'S HEAD

Difficult to find the way to Athens
without hooves to gallop on down the steps
of the British Museum. A boy stops
with his notebook and a box of coloured pens
to learn to draw you, plundered monument
of the exhausted empire. He opens
the box of pens and stares. He's not content

to draw your head on the marble pedestal;
it is the entire horse he sees: the stallion
never sculpted, pulling a champion
out of the sea, with bronze spear armed for battle,
a chariot with a single bronze wheel,
and two short, sturdy legs for you to run on.
Out you'll go in his notebook. For a while

the boy will hang you on his locker door.
But by the time he's twelve, something he heard
his teacher say about perspective, a word
or two about learning to draw what's there
will make him take the dog-eared paper down.
Back to the museum he'll come and stand here
to draw a horse's head of abraded stone.

APHRODITE OF MELOS

Never was a Hollywood starlet so
seized by spotlights in the gallery as
you, stone diva, by tourist cameras.
No screen goddess would ever have dared to
appear this composed in public—until
she cultivated dreamy ideas
about romantic evenings with a pill.

To bear the gaze without a smile is death:
rising stars cannot afford detachment.
At the final rehearsal, her agent
smiled a salt-white smile. She gathered her breath
and quipped a one-liner his hack composed.
To memorize twenty seconds, she spent
hours of mirror-practice carefully posed

and became a paper Venus. Picture
her skin reflecting the rose of crimson
sheets, her blond hair fanned across the satin,
hung on the wall, part of the furniture
in a basement temple. Makes you wonder
whether the dead are better served by stone
than by a million monuments of paper.

JORDAN

1.

The Jordan Curve Theorem states that any closed non self-intersecting loop describes exactly two regions: the inside and the outside. Everything not inside the loop is outside. Everything not outside the loop is inside. Skeletal proof by contradiction: suppose a closed non self-intersecting loop defines no region. Then it would be possible to draw a path between any two points without colliding with or crossing the loop. At any point on the loop, draw a short perpendicular crossing line. Draw two points on the perpendicular close to but on opposite sides of the loop. It is impossible to draw a line between these two points that the loop does not intersect (follow the loop around in your head).

2.

If every material thing is finite
in space and time
the mind
can enclose it with sufficient string.
The Jordan River,
extended south to the Red Sea,
north through underground streams
long forgotten
to the Scamander,
along the Mediterranean coast
to the Nile
creates a closed non self-intersecting
loop around Palestine, Israel, Lebanon,
Gaza, Sinai.

IRIS

Who planted a single root of white iris?
A gardener with a sense of humour
or a patient with an eye for colour?
It may have been an asylum guest. Did this
iris bloom before the others in May,
the tentacle root tapping ground water,
early candidate for a bright bouquet?

Was this a mistake, a bulb of the white
variety misplaced in a bushel
of blue, bearded irises? A petal
cannot express its colour in its root.
Were bees to throng above the violent stems,
they would fly over this flower and fill
with pollen from blue beards and golden mums.

Vincent, the solitary bloom of the white
iris droops from the stem. A late winter
frost singed the shallow root. The cold weather
favours more deeply rooted bulbs. The weight
of the dew wilts a petal to the root
as a suicide surveys the water,
concentrating a last moment of thought.

Photographer on the Steps
of the National Gallery

From here, I can't will into motion
the Trafalgar pigeons,
hoping the mole-mouth aperture
and slow-to-close shutter

will expose the fluttering blur
of their collective flight.
A postcard saves embarrassment
and time—enough to meditate on the hare

bounding ahead of the steam
train on a Turner canvas.
The hare will leap across the ties
until the engine overtakes him

and he lies low under the rolling cars
or leaps a last leap into the spinning gears.

Mountain Prayer

for Peter Van Toorn

O carnadine cryptographer!
O disenchanted char chanter!
O rhyme receipt, recipe for riot!
O alphabet elf supreme!
O small-framed fame chaser!
O barrel-chested behemoth tasting chimes!
O imagiste intellect!
O titan tobacco toker! Tone toddler!
O saxophone sarcasmaddict!
O tabernac bard, time out for word snack!
O whale talker, tailor of tun!
O surefooted looter of the word horde!
O phrase ferret stuck on phlegm!
O unlicensed limner locked up!
O grass grazing foal bolus!
O tin man! Timbre tinker!
O poetry pastry! Pam! Pam! Pam!
O bawdy mind in organized song!
O tanka zen Tarzan!
O temporal Poe, tempus fidgeter!
O pure cure of descant disease!
O marked maker moniker monger!
O zenith of pizzazz and schmaltz!
O mustang maker maxing out!

That being said,
his nibs' nose's pressed to the grass
for old time's sake,
maybe trying to
trip out
on maple root

or shoot a foot in the door
of that old school.
Large lungs,
undertaken,
cavities for smoke and wind—
more than blows across an Adirondack peak!—
no telling what prize the wind
hides for those of you who ride her back
most recklessly.
He's dropped a line or two
to remember him by.
An inventive father,
fathered by an inventor,
father of poets in every corner of the city,
strung out on
nothing that couldn't be shaken down
riding the mind like the wind
with open ears,
unsaddled, bridle-
less—
just a book of dreams to climb on
and look out
like Cézanne
that mountain man.
Still, no tears for peers.
Let my daughter's days be filled with crayons
and paper enough to draw her days out
with a word of praise.
A rumour that starts in the earth
comes home,
stays in tune like a stone harp.

The wind pulls up
from time to time
just as it pushes out.
It pushes me as it pulls you
and rises like a daughter
every morning
somewhere back of all these pines.

THE ROCKING HORSE

His toy-box kingdom would he give for an ear.
In the rocking chair was no mimesis. His mother
in it held and fed him while he pulled her hair.
No horse, this toy of foreign manufacture,
this site solitary of joust imaginary.
In it he mimics—no, mocks—Bellerophon:
in plastic saddle, nylon mane, no chivalry.
The past alone he would have the present built on;

a past when, as the breaker of horses rode,
the laurels fell upon his head like snow.
Never was then a lack of milk or food.
Then did the reader read and praise bestow.
The springs, white-rusted, make music with his voice
(that in pitch rises, in tempo quickens)
and keep the wingless courser in its place
while, jittery, rocks the hyperactive horseman.

It creaks away the hours of imagined youth
on oxidizing springs until the little horseman
falls off out of spite, shrieking through milk teeth,
dismounted, the one-metre sovereign.
But, re-employed, his mother's not home yet.
His caregiver can't hear a thing outside;
she's holding in the last drag on a cigarette.
Who did it hurt to let the rider, solo, ride?

O how the mites and centipedes welcome
the spider's Trojan horse to attic or garage!
Each plastic nostril a nest, each crevice a home:
covered it is, now, with web and carapace.

Decrepit, discovered by new tenants,
in trash thrown, in landfill dumped, it decays
as patiently as words and covenants,
with a half-life measured by centuries.

EVOLUTIONS

Bell in a Vacuum

Without air, the bell
oscillates
but will not ring.
The parishioners
measure the sun's height,
marking the carillon's absence;
the deaf boy on the hill
recalls the bell's resonance in his ribs,
feeling nothing;
not one motley pigeon
flies from the belfry.

The sexton hangs from the rope
with his right hand;
incensed by the silence,
he tears his hair with his left.
His mouth gapes, the uvula,
a too-short clapper,
dangles; the tongue,
too soft, garbles his curse.

But the iron mallet bulb does
shake the bronze bell;
look closely:
you can see the blurred
image of the vibrating bell
if your eye is quick
and as long as light reflects.

Monique

Monique (what compels me to name
the anonymous dead?)
caught the plague and died
bravely on a bed not of thatch.
We found her buried in the bog
with remarkable possessions.
The plastic shell of a music box
that helped her sleep.
Brightly coloured acrylic
wool and two glass
beads, the remains of a doll
she must have held for comfort.
A faded purple bangle,
her favourite colour.
The soles of a pair of shoes
she may have danced in.
A flaked, nickel-plated beret
she wore in her hair
(from what we know her hair was black).
The perfectly preserved
glass of a frame that may have held
a long-decomposed
photograph of her family.
Her father lay beside her in this other
simple grave.
His bones remained
to identify the shared genetics of their ancestry.
Where under the earth her mother lies
we have little hope of knowing.

The History of Scribes

The ideal scribe
has no understanding
of the content of a message.
The king selects the scribe
for his ability to transcribe
words exactly as spoken,
for never alerting the king
to accidental irony,
for his concern for the beauty of the text
not for his ideas.
It is said the king's trusted scribe Nasul
transcribed his own death sentence.
Loyal in matters of the text,
beautiful, naïve Nasul
seduced the king's
daughter in her royal chambers.
His sentence read exactly as follows:
Ima hanta hasi ol siman nasul ponti holotle.
The untranslatable
may be paraphrased:
I, Nasul, for violating the princess,
will cut off my hands.

Ivy and William

Ivy at the hurdy-gurdy,
William at the oud:
not the expected instruments.
Where between Lisgar High and here
were the guitar and keyboard lost?
No positive reinforcement for their fumbling
but a volley of overripe
fermenting fruit.
Ivy cannot bear the cat-in-heat
yowl of the hurdy-gurdy
much less identify a tune.
Five strings and no frets
render useless William's
practice on the pentatonic scales.
Who among us could find the mode
for an untempered scale
among so many hostile ears?
After this performance
uncertain the children's shelter,
certain their hunger.
What use the metronome?
What use the Mel Bay Method Book?
What use the digital tuner?
What use, Dr. Suzuki, your love?

Adrienne

She had never awoken
with a rat beside her; now
in the hold of a frigate
on the Atlantic mid-way
between Rouen and l'Acadie
the rats are the least of her worries.
She could never have imagined
that a woman would lie beneath a man
who grins like an ape fully clothed
in a tattered tunic, ten feet from a body
freshly abandoned
by the spirit in its blood.
She had never seen a corpse in Markham.
Adrienne and the babies scream; a dog
eats the last of the rotting salt pork;
rivulets of urine run
between port and starboard in the heavy seas.
On deck, the gale will bring no relief,
the exhausted crew will offer no comfort.
In six months, the winter snow will be familiar.
She will thank the old woman
who taught her how to keep a fire
burning through the night. God bless fire,
she will say to herself, hot
chocolate at the mall not a memory
but a distant, luxurious dream.

Increase Macdonald

To say that Increase Macdonald's mother
fretted over her son's uncertain future
would be in keeping with the understated
character of her Scottish ancestors.
She silently grieved in her sleep. She wept
in the bath quietly. If she had known
that long ago the Celts out-ululated
Saracens, she would have ululated
over tea for hours with the windows shut,
the blinds drawn, and the door locked. The boy's name
merits a few words. It is pronounced "In
Cree Us"—and if I've already offended,
God forgive me. It was the Christian name
of his grandfather and of his grandfather's
grandfather. Naming children never changes.
In the unprinted book of names a father
reads in troubled sleep while he rests his arm
on the taut appleskin of his wife's womb
every name has already been written.
None are removed. Not Adolf, not Nero.
Who would honour their first born with the name
of their Latvian great uncle Stalin
who survived a pogrom? The name in the book remains.
Those who believe they have penned a new name
read the Book to find that it is shared with
twenty, or one hundred, or ten thousand.
Over the birth of every second first
born son, grandfather Increase presides
to secure the delivery and name.
It would seem that no sin of tobacco,
no excess of gin, no disease, no war,
no blink-of-an-eye-asleep-at-the-wheel

act of God, could put to an early rest
the hardy first born Macdonald sons.
To put it in the Old Testament tongue
every Increase Macdonald recites,
"Increase begat John, Michael, William
and Eliza. John begat Increase
and Mary. Michael begat Increase
and Eleanor. Increase begat John,
Stephen, Bruce, Elizabeth and Mary.
John begat William and Harold. Stephen
begat Increase, Quinn, Leila and Kay."
Today, Good Friday, Increase Macdonald,
son of Quinn and Claire, returned from New York
with two perfect rows of transplanted baby's teeth.

Pitches

The ∞ Switch

Eliminate forever your fears of inadequate network capacity.
With no limit on point-to-point gamma-ray interfaces, this
switch is capable of supporting all future traffic; its billions of
ports can interconnect

> If starlight for a moment
> stopped—would there be time
> to think

everything. Add a dialogue simulation engine; your customers
will be able to record automated conversations and play them
back during free time. Unlimited, lifetime

> of another life. Still
> I recall my grandfather
> hands and face rough.

capacity voice and data mailboxes guarantee no one will ever
lose an important message. Address the customer's need for
immediate

> He was a cat's tongue
> smelling of oil and—what was it?—
> turpentine.

intimacy; install our graviton-gain capacitor to correct network
latency on interplanetary calls. Connect yesterday with The ∞
Switch from Azlon.

THE ALLTOY PLAYALL

Child's play should not be limited by time, space, or personal
finance. Consider the freedom of the ultimate toy. Download
your child's favourite extrusion model from the millions

      My mother told us stories
      of grass that grew for miles
      and of stones

at our universal web site. Refresh the polyperithane wells and
watch as the toy materializes before your child's gratified eyes.
Don't fret needlessly about the environment; place

      that grew from the earth like grass
      so heavy they were carried
      away by boats.

forgotten or disused Alltoys in the reconstitution cylinder. Not
only will you help to reduce the extent of the fill; you'll
continually stimulate your child. You'll even cut

      Before my brother died
      I had no word for grief
      I could not form the letters.

down on the cost of polyperithane!

FUTURE PIZZA

At 2 am on Saturday morning, don't you want your pizza
without bothering to order it? Our patented routing algorithms,
portable

> Why do we no
> longer eat from
> the earth?

ovens, and extensive behaviour databases ensure that we
deliver piping pizza on time, at the very moment

> Mothers and babies
> were said to eat from it.

you want it. Looking for a change of taste? Let the deliverer
customize the pizza with up to five ingredients.

> Was it for iron
> or for some natural salt
> that folic acid
> could not substitute?

Don't want your pizza tonight? Don't worry. Our next customer
will love it!

EVERYDROID FLOWERBOTS

A clean gardener is an admired gardener and gardening has
never been so clean. Imagine arranging the perfect flower
garden using your personal information manager and our
responsive cellulonitinol flowerbots any time

> I want a pear
> that decays from the outside in,
> grapes whose must
> ruins a vintage.

of day. Choose from hundreds of species, colours, sizes, aromas,
and petal configurations. Impress

> I want to bury my nose
> like a muzzle in un-
> irradiated meat.

your friends by developing personalized flowers—a giant lotus
that smells like a rose! For a few more credits, try our
heliotropes—make the tallest, brightest

> If you want me to love you
> do not bathe.

sunflowers ever seen. Imagine the pleasure of a winter noon
walking in the sun among your sunflowers and
chrysanthemums. Make that peonies and poppies!

Evolutions

After one hundred years no ant
will shuttle across a bedroom floor.
After one thousand years no hare
will bound across lake ice in November.
After ten thousand years no roadside porcupine
will weigh less than four hundred kilos.
In one hundred thousand years no man
will kill, although a few may dream of it as others
will dream of green fields and have no teeth to grind.

FRUITFLY
GEOGRAPHIC

Tiger Lily

Grass cannot grow
      tall enough
to cover

the fire bulb
of the tiger lily.

      The black
fleck on the petal
      names the species.

A Jar of Gasoline

Fire rises in a field
hidden from the road
by a tangle of hawthorns.
To conquer
fear by lighting fire,
a boy holds a jar of gasoline,
afraid to let it fall;
his friends watch him.
As the column of flame
climbs to the jar,
      a voice
             calls. Heat
cracks the glass in his hand.

WEEDS

Crack and spring
from the concrete, weeds.
Steal one hour of sun
from high windows at noon.

Bloom between sidewalk and street,
hidden from pedestrian feet.
Burst from flowers
into urban breeze your seeds.

Bees love you; they too
abandon
nothing. Under the eaves
they build their hives.

In the sun-baked air
outside the air-conditioned car,
your flowers provide them
pollen grains to feed on.

THOOR BALLYLEE IN JANUARY

The palm
sucks the damp
stone

set by a Norman mason,
inscribed by the Irish bard—

no; inscribed by a Galway
stone cutter,

each character chiselled
from an outline
drawn in chalk.

An old arthritis
blooms in the wrist.

Deer, Beaver, Buck, Bull

1.

The deer should spring
back into the bush
when it sees my new bronze Buick
reflect the early morning sun.
But without lifting a hoof from the grass,
its eyes follow the car;
its head turns on the sunflower
stalk of its neck.

2.

Under the overpass
efficient passage
between streams
concerns the beaver;
the reverberating din
of six half-litre cylinders
earns no glance from eyes
fixed like an agent
on future values.

3.

A buck and a bull moose:
face-to-face trophies
in my uncle's
A-frame cottage.
Their glass eyes,
dull as empty apostrophes,
signify neither possession
nor dialogue.

ABSENCE OF THE BOBOLINK

Watch the growing
          heat of the summer fields:
clasped by the grass,
          listen for its *pink pink*.

If not for bees and crickets,
          in its absence
you would find
          a paradise of silence.

Scan the crop in this
          disregarded field:
the purple clusters
          of loose-strife

subdue the violet
          heads of dry clover.
If the rumour is true,
          the black widow

has discovered
          southern Ontario.
In an abandoned field
          north of The Pas

the bobolink bends
          a stem of scrub grass.

April Violin

He plays violin
on the Bronson Street
                    overpass
concrete abutment
ignorant of the traffic
dissonance
silencing his strings.
Street dust
spirals in the
            wake of cars,
gathers at his feet.
One sustained tone
escapes the rioting
                    crowd
            of rush-hour traffic
under the overpass.

Furze

Furze and the flesh of a peach were found
in the mouth of Deirdre.
Off the Malone road children brawl
like Dublin cats on a garden wall:
fiercely, with prize-fighting claws
the size of steeples. The boots of an angel
imprint the mud with the lip and bowl
of an urn near the footpath's discarded fag.
Cobble, corner, key, and flag
flecked with the ash of persistent coal.

ANTS

Close up, the children watched
more than one
burn in the magnified
beams of the sun.

Black ants burned with the scent
of spoiled cherries;
they gathered the nectar
from flowering trees.

Red ants burned with the wild
must of the earth;
they were fed on the dead
from birth.

Black Truffle

Nothing on the tongue more subtle; from the earth,
not of it; of garlic, clove, oak, air
and stars if stars were small enough to taste
and sprinkle on risotto.

With difficulty cultivated under
hundred-year-old oak as the Californian
knew: replaced fifty acres of sequoia
to make a grove from topsoil, loam

and seedling oak, shipped from Provence across
an ocean and a continent by steam,
so his grandson could sell the fungal pearls
to gourmets in San Francisco.

Rare as honest speech, the best of these poems
of oak from earth are not harvested but
discovered by a farmer's hungry pig.
No reverence or commerce checks

its desire to devour the tuber whole.
Watch the farmer swing a barbed switch
to keep the muzzled snout
from bruising what it cannot eat.

Autumn Leaves

By the end of October our maple
has dropped another hundred thousand leaves.
Year after year I cart bag after stuffed
paper bag from the backyard to the curb.
Let them rot. I am sick of the emeralds
of the gaudy summer grass. Let the strongest
flower rise through the spring leaf-quilt
like a Saturday morning erection.
Neighbour, you who rake your lawn,
you are a messenger for the end of days,
delivering the junkmail leaves that beg
"Buy fresh, buy new before all this decays."

Dining in Eden

Eve spiced well the breath of Adam:
cumin, coriander, onion,
tomato, almond and vine.

Adam spiced well the breath of Eve:
basil, tarragon, garlic,
eggplant, walnut and fig.

Hand to mouth they fed, washed
with water from the unnamed
source of the Euphrates.

The tongue hungers
more than it longs to name.

STONE IN THE FIELD

Violent the breaking of stone:
the thunderclap of the impact
shatters the handle,

disperses shards,
shakes the hand's bones.

Mineral stars emerge from the granite
on the grass in scattered pieces.

The Fruitfly

The veins on the fruit fly's wings map the rivers
of a small corner of Minnesota and Ontario
as they may have flowed or yet may flow.

Out of fruit, out of nothing, the fly beats its wings
a thousand thousand times before hands clap it
not into history, for that would take a scrawl

darker and longer than its 6 point semi-colon
rinsed from the palms, but into diminishing silence.
Let's say the first molecule of air to be unmoved

by its high-pitched harmony marks its end.
By then bananas, mangos and papayas,
pomegranates, quinces and figs, all feared

exotic fruit will burst from their nothings
generations of possible geographies.

NOTE

Three Deaths of Hippasus of Metapontum: Pythagoras of Samos
travelled widely before establishing a "school" at Croton, a
village on the south-eastern coast of Italy. Pythagoreans
believed that whole numbers and their ratios were, in effect,
the elementary particles of nature. This belief was based on
evidence—the ratios of musical scales, the proportions of
astronomical observations—and on Pythagoras' unquestioned
authority as leader of the sect (members of the school spoke
"the master said so" to affirm apparently self-evident truths).
Hippasus, a member of the school, is believed to have
discovered the existence of irrational numbers, a contradiction
of Pythagorean doctrine. He may have chanced upon
irrational numbers while contemplating the Pythagorean
theorem: the square of the length of the hypotenuse of a right
angle triangle is equal to the sum of the squares of the lengths
of the other two sides. For sharing his discovery, he was said to
have been drowned at sea, poisoned or exiled. We have only
fragmentary accounts; the Pythagoreans, to guard their
secrecy, wrote little that survives.

Acknowledgements

Thanks to the irreverent Peter van Toorn for his reverence for poetry, to Nicole for her emotional complexity, to Mathieu for his gift of humour, to Danica for her gift of perpetual surprise, to rob mclennan for his cleverly disguised honesty, to Ken Norris, Peter Norman, Melanie Little, Laurie Fuhr, Anita Dolman, James Moran, Ronnie Brown, Jeffery Donaldson, Stuart Ross, and Danny Wall for reading.

Some of these poems are in memory of Kathleen Frank who was one of their first and most perceptive readers, and Marc Gauthier who was their inspiration.

Thanks to Michael Holmes and ECW Press for generosity and unapologetic eclecticism.

Thanks to the editors of the following journals and small presses for first publishing some of these poems: *Antigonish Review*, *Another Toronto Quarterly*, *Arc*, *blue moon*, Delirium Press, *Danforth Review*, *Drunken Boat*, *Fiddlehead*, *It's Still Winter*, *The Lantern Review* (Ireland), *Maisonneuve*, *Marin County Poems* (above/ground press, Ottawa, 2001), *The New Delta Review*, *Paperplates*, *Prairie Fire*, *Queen St Quarterly*, *Short Fuse: New Fusion Poetry* (Rattapallax Press, N.Y., 2002, Todd Swift and Philip Norton), *Vintage 2000*.